The Daydreaming Mogul's Guide Volume 2:

Credit Score Dating
The Sexiness of Credit

Niem M. Green

The Daydreaming Mogul's Guide Volume 2: Credit Score Dating – The Sexiness of Credit

ISBN 9780988965904
Library of Congress Control Number: 2016900646
Printed in USA

For you, your heart, and your love, my unicorn. What has been spoken of, yet dificult to see, fore it is you that has truly inspired me. May this guide that you've mused prove gratitude beyond what the eye can see. Always and forever from now through eternity.

Contents

Foreword

I first learned about Niem Green and Creditscoredating.com this past February through an article in the Wall Street Journal. As a subject matter expert in financial education and the importance of it to all we do, I cleaned up my LinkedIn profile and sent Niem an invite to speak.

What I wasn't prepared for was Niem himself! His belief in and love for what he does just jumps off the page. He talked about his algorithm (without revealing the secret sauce), his ideas, the importance of educating people about credit and their financial lives and where hopes this can go.

Then I learned about Daydreaming Mogul….and acting your dreams out with open eyes. And then how much children mean to Niem and the work he is doing for children, Young Daydreamers.

His energy and passion never cease to amaze me. But through this all Niem remains focused, grounded and principled. For Niem, it's all about helping people live their lives to the fullest. And he gets that point across all the time…every time!

I won't say Niem is hardworking; he is what he does. He IS the Daydreaming Mogul; he IS CreditScoreDating.com; he IS Young Daydreamers. He truly IS!

Niem truly loves what he is doing and the change he can bring. He is someone you're glad to have met and proud to know, someone you want to lead your team.

It's the hope that everything you read in The Daydreaming Mogul's Guide Volume 2: Credit Score Dating – The Sexiness of Credit. will lead you to a healthy romantic life.

We at the Financial Counseling Association of America (FCAA) are incredibly excited to be able to offer individuals the help they need to live healthy financial lives. Just as important as finding love is finding balanced financial footing.

There are no shortcuts to financial health or romantic happiness. It's all about focus, dedication and balance. If you need help getting back on track with your budgeting plans, our experienced FCAA member agencies can help you get back on track financially. Maybe it is working to pay off over burdened debt loads, build up your emergency reserves, or save for that dream vacation. No matter what the reason, we all want to see you live the lives you always dreamed you could.

Introduction

In life there are 2 things that will forever be in demand and forever depend on each other, they are relationships and finance. It doesn't matter what type of relationship, working, personal, or family, they all at some point or consistently involve and sometimes dissolve because of finance.

Hello again all it has been a while since I've had the pleasure of writing for you all. I'm Niem M. Green, CEO of the Creditscoredating.com, also referred to as "The Daydreaming Mogul". Now for my fans and readers from the first book in the series "The Daydreaming Mogul's Guide Vol. 1 Daydreams and Success", you know that I like to lay out a few disclosures before we get started. This time I'd like to do the same, however, it is a little different as I am as some would call a subject matter expert in the topic we will discuss in this book. While I've created the algorithm and trade secret behind the revolutionary site "Creditscoredating.com" that is matching singles up by financial compatibility, credit, and financial acumen, I am not a psychologist or psychiatrist for that matter. I am, however, a career trained credit analyst and underwriter. I have made decisions on countless credit applications from mortgage loans to credit cards and everything in between.

I have spoken with some of my associates in various industries. They have years of experience in their respective industries. I interviewed them to help you to understand the correlation between finance, credit, dating and relationships.

These include experts from Porsche and the auto industry. I've also sat down with a relationship therapist.

I own Creditscoredating.com, we match singles by their credit among other things. Sounds crazy right? Well maybe not so much, this is what I will discuss with you in this book. Our company's tagline is "Where Good Credit is Sexy" ™, and "It All Starts with a number" ™ this is what we will explore the "sexiness" of credit and why it all starts with a number. I know some of you are thinking "how in the world is credit sexy?" No worries, I have received that same response from countless reporters, talk show hosts, and the general public all over the world.

So let us get in to this shall we? Back to the opening statement, sometimes relationships dissolve because of finance. In fact, the leading cause of divorce and relationship turmoil has been finance or monetary issues. At the bank as an underwriter my job in its simplest terms was to determine the relationship with the potential borrower. In fact, in many cases this determination is made in 90 seconds or less. In essence, as an underwriter, I was a matchmaker. I had to determine the likelihood of "divorce" or default if we were to extend credit to that borrower. In personal relationships, singles date to find that "right one." Through the courting or dating process, they determine the likelihood of "default" or divorce.

Now isn't this interesting? Did you know that while you were dating you were really underwriting to approve or deny for your love or time? Hold on, because we barely scratched the surface. By the end of this book, you will be equipped with a more refined knowledge of credit and its importance in life and relationships. You will also be what I like to call "relationship underwriters." Even if you are currently in a relationship, dating, or considering it, you will be equipped to look at things from a more analytical point of view which will help to better your odds at success in your relationships.

My goal is not to scare you from taking risks but to help you to understand the tools to better calculate said risks. It is also very important that I clarify that wanting good credit or a mate with good credit does not make you "gold digger." We will talk about this further in later chapters, I will say this, in hundreds of thousands, possibly millions of applications and credit reports I've analyzed, I've noticed that some people with higher scores had lower incomes than those with higher incomes. It appeared that people with lower incomes with good credit were conditioned to spend and budget within and below their means. The people with higher incomes seemed to live above and have a higher reliance on credit. Again, we will discuss this further in later in this book.

The goal of this book much like my dating site is to educate. While I may be accredited by my degree, my experience in lending, and even my site. I want you all to take this advice and my accreditation into consideration not as a businessman and public figure who has spoken throughout the world or been in major news and on TV globally. Simply as a fellow consumer who has had bad credit and good, great relationships and absolutely horrible relationships.

The thing in common about both situations in regard to credit and relationships, is the ignorance, that is, lack of information and knowledge. My losses become your gains, my failures become your successes with this book.

Strap on your seat-belts and prepare to be educated and entertained on this rollercoaster ride of love, finance, and credit score dating, "Where Good Credit is Sexy." ™ Because, "It All Starts with a Number." ™

Chapter One

"Initial Feeling"

You've been looking for the perfect match, you've heard your friends, family and co-workers talking about it. This may be your first time, maybe you've had others. Possibly the last relationships ended badly, maybe they ended on more positive terms. Nonetheless, you're starting to give up, in fact people are telling you, "you can't look for it, it'll happen when you stop looking." You think, "that's easy to say when you have found your perfect match." Licensed Psychotherapist, Kier A. Berkel of New Castle, DE simplifies this as "People need people."

Finally, it happens, you meet someone that seems to satisfy everything in your criteria. They answered every question right, they had the right tone, their approach was correct. It is that "Initial Feeling", you're enamored. You think that this must be what you've been waiting for the entire time. This person was made just for you, thus, they are the perfect match.

This is the initial feeling that we felt as under-writers also, "Oh yeah, they're approved." Their application looks correct, their credit report looks good, their credit score fit within the approvable guidelines, and they answered everything just right. However, we could have been wrong, much like in meeting someone new. A new applicant for credit is much like a new applicant for courtship. We often put our best foot forward when meeting new people, especially when something we want is on the line. We're taught at an early age that "first impressions are everything."

"We don't have to be taught to want to socialize, it's usually innate. If we have a good upbringing, when we're born, if we have that nurturing that we need it's already pre-programed in us to be social creatures. So it's nothing that we have to really think about, although we make it complicated, it is naturally within us." - Kier

My fellow co-workers and I used to call some of these applicants "career applicants." They would go from bank to bank to study application processes to find out what questions would be asked and what the application processes would be, that is, how strenu-ous or how easy the applications were.

These applicants were easy to spot after a while, they seemed to good to be true. They knew the right answers; they knew bank jargon even. They would even cite acronyms that I would otherwise only hear in the bank.

While it is true that a percentage of these applicant may have been versed in the process, and possibly may even have had lending backgrounds, the majority had not. How did we know the difference? What was the telltale? Their credit file didn't add up. For example, why were they on the phone with me in the first place? Well, typically if you find yourself on the phone with an underwriter for a credit card, it is for one of two reasons, either verification, something needs to be verified address, phone, etc. or they need clarification of something credit related.

The other telltale was the number of inquiries from credit card companies in one period of time. If there are many at one time, it is possible that it is fraud, however, that is an entirely different "talk show", so I'll save that for another book and time.

Now how does this relate to dating? I'm sure you're wondering. Have you ever met someone and they seem to be perfect and answer everything correctly, yet something just doesn't add up? Let's apply the same credit applicant to a dating scenario.

The suitor, man or woman, is perfect, from their personality to their smile. They answer all of your questions perfectly, almost as if they've practiced the night before. (They probably have, just on a different person, ok, ok I'll hold my cynicism.) However, you start to talk about their past relationships or dating experiences. Could be later that evening or on another date, and they tell you a long list of people who it didn't work with. It could possibly be just the last relationship they were in that it did not work with. Nonetheless, it is 1 of 2 things, the other person's fault or "mutually they've decided it to split on good terms."

This is what we'll call a "career dater," they've found the sweet spot how they can best answer the question that everyone seems to get "You're so great, why are you single?" without looking bad.

Think of that episode of Seinfeld, when George used the picture of Jerry's girlfriend along with the story that his ex-fiancé died. This is the same philosophy, of course the show used the comical approach, nevertheless, career daters try to find the correct answers and group of circumstances that will incite the interest of the person they're trying to date.

I joined Dagen Mcdowell of Fox Business News and Fox News, for a news segment in which she stated;

"I can tell you how you can identify this without no offense to Niem, without using his service. If you go out with a guy and he spends a lot of money on your very first date, that is a trouble sign. Or if the person dresses in a way that is to expensive for the job he has."

One thing I will say that I've learned over the years, is not to cast judgment. I am however analytical by nature and by trade. With that being said, I'm sure it is possible that there are people out there who some how manage to date a lot without wrongdoing. However, what are those odds? Seriously, those would have to be very small odds. We are imperfect, I am no exception, I'm sure there are a few people who would tend to agree. With our imperfections and being creatures of habit, it takes a few tries sometimes to get things correct. Relationships and dating are no exception. You can't appreciate the best if you've never experienced the worst. We can't perfect something without making mistakes, hence, the saying "practice makes perfect." Dating and relationships are no exception, we have to learn and grow individually as well as in relationships to perfect our interpersonal interaction, skill, and competencies.

If there were this "perfect" flawless person out there with a 100% dating percentage. I'm almost certain they are in a serious relationship or married. Even Beyoncé, who made the song "Flawless" is married.

I took a bit of a lighthearted approach to the matter just to break the ice. The point is still the same, however, to remember is the "initial feeling." While yes, the initial feeling is a great one, the key to keeping the relationship fresh is to recreate the initial feeling. Be cautioned that there is another initial feeling that we sometimes do not pay attention to or take heed, that is one of caution and risk factors. "If it seems to good to be true, it probably is." This is the old saying, and it's an old saying that is passed from parent to child amongst families and generations for good reason.

Sometimes not taking heed to cautionary "initial feeling" is like approving a bad loan. The one thing in underwriting that is worse than approving a bad loan is not asking the proper questions to prevent from approving a bad loan.

Bad loans happen, that's a part of life and part of the lending world and environment. As in relationships, there will be break ups and bad relationships, that is a part of life. Again, this is a part of our growth, maturity, and learning how to manage our relationships. There are many variables and forces that affect both, loans and relationships. We will touch on this in a later chapter, however, worse than being in a bad relationship is not trying to prevent it.

Would you purposely put yourself in the worst situation ever? Of course not, yet this is what we do when we do not take heed to the cautionary initial feeling.

At the bank I would see other underwriters try to meet their goals of approval rates by not doing illegal things but by not paying attention to their cautionary "initial feelings." What would happen is that their approval rates would be high but their legacy, or accounts that they've approved over time, default rates would become higher. The end result became the same and it was never good for the bank, the borrower, or the underwriter.

Applying this to relationships, if we just look at the "glittering" of being in a relationship and not pay attention to the cautionary initial feeling and take the time to understand why it is there and investigate, the end result is often the same. One or both people in the relationship are hurt and unfortunately, if there are children involved they are hurt also.

Often times after relationships suffer and turn for the worst, the parties typically say, "I never knew he or she was like that, it was like they turn into a different person." Yet, the signs were there the entire time. In a lot of cases we tend to turn a blind eye to these things or ignore the cautionary "initial feeling" because of what we want or what we feel we "need." We "need" to be with someone, we "need" to find a wife or husband, we don't "need" to sleep alone anymore. Our kids "need" a mother or father, we "need" to have kids, etc. Much like my fellow underwriters, they "need" to meet their approval goals, the "need" to get their bonuses, etc. There is every incentive to overlook the cautionary initial feeling for the good initial feeling.

Another old saying, "haste makes waste" my mother and grandmother, used to say this to me all the time. This can certainly be applied here also in both scenarios. If we hastily rush to make decisions, jump in relationship, make approvals, etc. what do we end up with? We waste our time, our careers in some cases, end up with broken hearts, etc.

Part of the blame still lies on us also, by looking at what we feel we need without evaluating our strengths or weaknesses. In some cases, we know but we ignore this also. I'm not talking about the superficial or surface things. Sure that beautiful person who is compatible on "paper". You 2 may even have the best photos ever and can imagine the beautiful baby together. However, what about this person matching with you on the worst day. How do they react to the some of your flaws, behaviors, or whatever things you may not admit to others?

My aunt used to prepare me financially for things I wanted. She would say, "Yeah, you have money in your pocket and your account, so things look easy to afford. But what about that bad day when there's an unexpected expense or even you got a little to happy and overspent? Can you afford it? If you can afford it on your worst day in the worst of circumstances, then go ahead and buy it." My Aunt Michelle will tell you, I didn't always listen and it took a while to catch on. This isn't because of any disability, it's simply that I am human and the "initial feeling" caught me several times.

There is great value in this and it can be applied to relationships also. Think of all you know of the person you're with and the worst scenario you experienced. Now granted, some of you are in relationships and may have been through bad experiences. How did you and your mate fair? Did this cause a disturbance in your relationship or life? If you aren't in a relationship or haven't experienced any issues like I'm describing, how do you think the person you are dating or considering will manage? Do you feel there are some signs in them or you that will conflict or escalate an already bad situation?

In some cases, we assess certain things about a person and say, yeah I can conform or they will. What happens if you can't or they won't? Remember, we are looking at the worst scenario and placing this person in it. With that being said, stress and pressure has a habit of changing people. So if normally a person would be receptive to your requests, comments, criticism, etc. the stress may cause a different response.

This all goes back to paying attention to both "initial feelings". The same is true for us in underwriting. In some cases we have to look to see if an applicant would be approvable in a certain situation. This could be good or bad, it could be our approval would have broken them and turned them into a risk. I will talk more about this a little later. We see why it's important to really pay attention to what "initial feeling" is stronger and investigate why it is there.

"People do research on the car they want. But they don't look at the back end of it. They look on the surface but don't look in depth of their purchase. Similarly, in dating people look at the looks and personality, everything at a surface level. But as the relationship develops and becomes more serious, they learn who this person is at the wrong times. Like when buying a car and were expecting that their partner was compatible with them financially, but they weren't. They feel they were deceived, it's risky. This is why people need to take that step and precautions to make sure they know who they are dating are they compatible with you financially." – Sean Johnson, General Manager, Porsche Delaware

"We want to exaggerate that image that the per-

son has already perceived. *Let's think of a young lady who's graduating from high school. She's getting notice, she's getting attention. Her foundation is telling her, "a man is not going to want you if you don't act like a lady, you have to act feminine. If you like sports that's cool but play that down a little bit, because that's really not what a man is looking for." Same thing for men, "you've got to really, really be masculine about it. Grow some facial hair, wear Timberlands you know, engage yourself in things society thinks are masculine." We don't teach the younger generations about being themselves. It's all about getting that man or that woman, getting that application, or getting that deal. So that's where the deception comes from in my opinion, because we are brought up with these perceptions that are just lies. We carry it throughout our lives into our dating world, into our career world, all of these perceived ideas of what people want."* – Kier Berkel

Chapter Two

New Era of Dating

This is a new world of everything, it is a time of advanced technology. We literally have the entire world in our hands. However, this is also a time of what Kier calls "instant gratification", a time when everyone wants what they want when they want it. That time is often now, "not now, but right now." This is for purchases, big or small, one time or recurring, careers, and even relationships.

It is hard to imagine there was a time that a person had to wait up to a minute to connect to the internet using dial-up. I can still remember the sound of the modem dialing into AOL. My daughter often laughs at me when I tell her stories of this and other things that seem like impossibilities to her. Just as to me it is hard to imagine there was a time when to speak with a loved one across the country or world, you would have to wait weeks, months, or years.

Try telling a jealous girlfriend that one, "Hey

babe, I'll be back, but I'll write you, so you'll hear from me every 6 - 12 months." With the right or wrong girlfriend or significant other more than likely you would not leave or you would not leave alone.

This poses a good question, jealousy in relationships, has technology influenced this or has does it help with this? Is there just cause for this or does it add to the high relationship turnover rates? With the rise of social networks, the world seems to be a buffet of "selfies", personal or overstated information, etc. Frivolous relationships seem to be on the rise and fall (break ups) also and the world knows about it all, thanks to social media and camera phones.

This seems to be the new way of relationships;

Like a picture on a random social media site

Post a witty comment or two with a cute emoji

Direct message your number

Text a simple "WYD" (What You Doing)

Arrange time to meet for casual date

Eventually have sex

Argue followed by break up

Like a new picture and repeat process

Now this may be a little extreme and I pray I didn't just describe your routine and if I did, please find a new one. However, this is where we seem to be, quick relationships that lack substance. I grew up with meeting people online when I was younger, which was exciting. This may be part of why I developed an interest in the online dating business.

Online dating is not a bad thing, in fact online dating is great especially for those with busy schedules or those who don't wish to meet people in bars and other places. I also say that online dating allows for singles to connect with and become attracted to a person's personality. Whether it's the creativity of a profile or the witty reply to a message, we are seeing a person's personality. Quickly we move past just seeing someone profile picture and move into learning about their mind or personality.

There are people who have different complexes, fears, and inabilities that prohibit them to show their true self in an offline environment. While yes, there are people who take the online approach to far, I.e.

"Catfishing" and other forms of deception and false personas. Yet, there are many people who genuinely find online dating as a safe haven and place to be and display "themselves" and hope to meet people to accept them for who they are.

Similarly, car buyers have used these advancements to make car purchases. Cars are typically the second largest purchase for the average consumer. "Car buyers come in as I call them "prepared." They know exactly what the want with all the specifications and price of the car before they meet with me." Brandon Rogers of Porsche Delaware explains. Brandon has years of experience as a sales consultant and has seen it all. "These buyers want what they want when they want it. They know everything from the color to the options they want. The only left is the price, that's what they meet with us about, essentially the car is sold before I first greet them."

This is again from the technological advancement allowing for customer to become "prepared".

There used to be a stigma of dating online however studies show that the stigma has and continues to fade away. In fact, online dating has become part of pop culture. According to Pew Research Center, in 2005 44% of Americans agreed that *online dating is a good way to meet people*. In 2013 the percentage increased to 59%. My thought is that this correlates with the advancement and greater access to technology. I believe that this correlates to Kier's theory of instant gratification and my thought of connecting with people's personalities while maintaining busy schedules.

If you look at some of the popular social networks and how they are being used, people are posting their lives, thoughts, feelings, views, etc. almost to a fault without demarcation. This makes it easier to connect with others without reservation and create a profile on an online dating site.

While the methods of connecting and meeting people may have changed or advanced, the problems of dating, relationships, and marriage have not. Relationships still end everyday, people are still filing for divorce, and singles still have reservations, fears, complexes, insecurities, etc. about relationships, dating, and committing. Money is still "the leading cause of stress in relationships" according to CNBC in a report published February, 2015.

With all the technological advances and why

have we not advanced as humans and singles to solve the money problem? What would be that solution? As I mentioned earlier in the introduction, my background is underwriting and analyst for banks. I also mentioned that I am the CEO of CreditScoreDating. com. I have and continue to refine the algorithm to address this question and find the solution. However, the solution, I've found over the years of running the site and working for various banks is very simple. The funny thing is, you don't have to be a data engineer, underwriter, or risk analyst to find the solution. The solution, much like most solutions in relationships, whether romantic, friendships, etc. lies in communication.

While my algorithm and site is able to and is designed to match singles by financial acumen and compatibility, the main goal is to get singles to discuss what they typically wont discuss until it is to late, the main cause of relationship stress and divorce, finance.

A lot of times, especially in the beginning of relationships, we talk and communicate. It's an exciting time, whether we are chatting with someone online or spending hours talking on the phone or texting throughout the day.

We want to know about this person, we love their voice, their laugh, their jokes, etc. We also want them to know about us, ironically we often leave out the most important things that will determine the length or the possibility of success in our relationships.

Now let me make the disclosure that I'm not talking about if you are not dating seriously or your goal is for "One Night Love" as my friends and I call it. This, much like the rest of this book and my site is for serious relationships.

Sometimes, however, we do get caught up in the physical, sexual, or mental attractions that we don't want to find reasons to end. This goes back to the previous chapter and the initial feeling.

With the advancement of technology, there is every temptation to ignore the cautionary initial feeling. Yes, there is a lot of temptations with easier access thanks to advances in technology, but we're just focusing on this one in particular.

With us putting so much of ourselves online, in all forms. We have more incentives to ignore our cautionary initial feelings. Whether it is because that person has lips that are so kissable, we can't wait to feel them or they seem like the perfect yin to your yang based on responses, posts, etc. you've observed. Just as Brandon explained with car buying, people are "prepared" in the online dating from the profile information, posts, likes, etc. They know about their potential mate before the first, "Hey, WYD, (What you doing?), message comes through.

I'm not exempt from this, I'm human, therefore I couldn't possibly say, "Don't do this, don't do that." I would be a hypocrite, in fact I love the advancement of technology and am appreciative of all it's done for me from personal to business and my career. I'm simply offering my advice to be cautious and know what we are up against when it comes to relationships and finding the correct one for us to be happy.

Chapter Three

"Til' Debt Do Us Part"

"Til' Debt Do Us Part" I know it seems like this would be the last chapter in a relationship book. I want to approach this from an analytical approach. As an underwriter at the bank, I was trained that credit was the first step of collections. The better job we do underwriting the easier job it would be for the collectors in the event the account went bad. The goal however, was to insure we did not approve an account that would not go bad. In relationships the better job we do at looking at what causes failure, the more effective we can be at success.

I mentioned that one of the main reasons that relationships fail is finance and the main cause for relationship stress is finance. That is very vague, in fact the topic of finance is very vague. In my career owning the site, from Creditscoredating.com to being an underwriter, I've heard it all. From spouses and significant others with spending problems to just not paying bills. However, one of the biggest financial issues plaguing relationships is "Debt."

According to the Fair Issac Corporation, the company that issue the FICO score, debt makes up 30% of the FICO score calculation. This is only second to payment history, which makes up 35% of the FICO score.

So why is debt so important to a score? For that matter, how can debt be such a burden to cause such a strain and turmoil on relationships? The short answer, it controls everything. Most importantly in relationships it controls "time and money" I'll explain that later. For now, and an even shorter answer, stress.

As an underwriter, one of the first things I looked at on an application and credit report is the debt to income ratio and the debt to credit ratio.

The first, debt to income ratio, would tell me how much financial stress the potential borrower was already under. A rule of thumb for me is to stay below 40% in fact 40% was a little on the high side depending on what type of product I was underwriting.

Think of when you applied for anything, credit

card, car, etc. and you list your income. What people typically list is their gross income (before taxes and deduction). The credit report will show your credit cards, car payments, mortgage, student loans, etc. What is not shown is your cell phone, utilities, rent, insurance, etc. So already the underwriter is not working with completely accurate information. This is why as an underwriter I wanted to make sure there was enough room for variables and misstated information.

The second ratio is the debt to credit ratio, often referred to as "utilization". This number is another financial stress indicator or potential stress. For example, if you have a credit card with a credit line of $1,000, and you typically revolve a balance of $500 and pay the minimum payment. This is your only card, this means your debt to credit ratio is 50%. This is high, this says that half of your credit available is used which can be an indication of higher risk. As an underwriter, I would look for around 30%.

Now I will say that in my time as an underwriter, things happen and a lot of times I would never rely on simply credit reports and numbers to make a decision. That is something that we will get into also in a later chapter. Most times I would talk to the borrower to determine the reason of indicated risk on the credit report or stress that would help with my decision. The point is debt has the ability to take a lot of if not most of our income, time to make income, and ultimately create stress if it is not controlled.

In speaking with one of the members of my site, she indicated that she and her ex never discussed credit until it was too late. When she learned of his credit issues which was debt, it was after she'd been married to the gentleman. The issue was he had a gambling addiction and he accumulated the debt from this. Naturally, this caused strain on their marriage and her personal finances which led to a divorce for the couple and a bankruptcy for her.

That member is just one of many stories I've heard over the years, I've heard some even worse. For example, debt of a member's now ex-spouse was accumulated because of drug and alcohol addictions. The problem was masked due to the ex's credit being exhausted so he was limited to what she, his wife could access, this him a functioning addict. When they married, he gained not only trust but access to credit. It wasn't long before he binged and their marriage and lives were completely destroyed.

Outside of these and other "worst case scenarios", debt is commonly accumulated and even under the best case scenario it can be stressful.

When you marry someone or even if you are in a serious relationship with someone you take one their debt. I'm not saying you it belongs to you legally or your credit reports merge, in fact that it is one of the biggest misconceptions of credit and relationships. However, when you plan a life with someone and you begin a family, naturally you share expenses and budget together. If I have $100,000 in debt and the future Mrs. Green has $100,000 in debt, we collectively have $200,000 in debt. It doesn't matter whose name it's in or how it's divided. I wouldn't want to be a part of the conversation telling a future wife "No I only have $20,000 in debt, you have $180,000 in debt, I don't know what you are going to do but I'm going to pay my $20,000 off and buy a sports car." I'm sure I would be single for a long time with that type of thinking.

The goal is to have a realistic and honest conversation about, what I call, "ghost of credit past, present, and future." Talk about what debt you have from the past, i.e. student loans, past relationships, etc. Talk about where you are currently, what are your current credit obligations, how many active credit cards do you have? How do you use them? How do you pay them? What is your car payment and / or mortgage payment? Finally, what are your plans, goals, and expectations for the future, what is your plans to pay those credit cards off? How about the loans and / or mortgage? He or she may be able to now understand that you are really serious about them but this is why you are always insisting that you both pay for yourselves on your dates. You can stop making excuses for getting out of dates or having date without spending money. Again, I'm joking, but seriously, if your serious about the person you are dating, work together, if one is lacking, make sure they are educated by the stronger.

This is a little ahead of ourselves, before we get to the plan of overcoming the problem that we've determined, let us determine it. In the introduction I indicated that you will be underwriters. Underwriters use tools to make an analysis of the borrower. Most of our tools are observations and questions.

I go back to my Aunt Michelle and her teachings. This is a great tool, self evaluation. Evaluate what you can or willing to handle and take on. This is not exclusively for finance, but also, in the relationship emotionally, mentally, romantically, etc. Apply real world scenarios to what your currently involved. If you've experienced them already, use this for litmus test to help. Look at your "Debt to Income" and "Debt to Credit" ratios, figuratively and literally. Can you take on more financial, emotional, or mental debt? How do you change in response to stress, good or bad?

I know I have dated women who transformed into completely different women under stress and pressure. I think of this visually as a scene from the movie "I'm Going to Get You Sucka". In the scene the leading actress was being pursued by 2 guys who wanted do her harm. Well in the film she had "cramps" it was her time of the month, if you will and she turned into a literal monster. While this was hilarious, I'm not saying women turn in to creature during their cycle. In fact, this depiction has nothing to do with the woman's cycle or not to sound misogynistic. I simply want to make the point that stress can cause a man or woman to turn into something completely different than what we know.

Conversely, sometimes stress cause people to rise to occasion and show a positive and more attractive side of them. Sometime we wont see that until they are in a situation that demands this transformation. I believe this part of our "fight or flight" response. The medical name for this is "acute stress response" as Walter Cannon, a scientist, neurologist, and physiologist, described in his 1915 theory, *"Bodily Changes in Pain, Hunger, Fear, and Rage: An Account of Recent Researches into the function of Emotional Excitement."*

Essentially when we experience stressful events, our bodies and minds react in 1 of 2 ways; either resist the event, or fight, or breakdown, or run away, flight. Sometimes, flight, causes people do have medical symptoms and cause illness mentally or physically. There is a lot medical research and information on this topic, again as I'm not a doctor, I can't delve in to deep. I just again want to give context to points to explain why we do some of the things we do. As well as, why we maybe should or shouldn't do things.

With all of this being said, evaluate what type of person you are, fight or flight. Are you fight, in financial stress while other stressors cause flight? Evaluate that in your partner or future partner. As I mentioned earlier, debt can cause stress, even indirectly. This is why it's important to have these discussions early on in the relationship.

Out of the millions of dollars in tools and software that the banks used that I worked for, the best tool I used that was the most effective was great conversation.

"Talking about money is still Taboo in our communities, I don't know why. What a person earns is a private matter, however, we should dispel that farce as well, because if you want to be with me we have to share money, if we have to pay these bills especially if we're going to have kids. We can't keep secrets about how much we make and how much we spend." - Kier

Chapter Four

"But What's Credit Have to Do with It?"

"Everything" – Sean Johnson General Manager, Porsche Delaware

Sean has been in the car sales industry and has seen it all. He explains how patterns he's observed in normal business are easily relatable to relationships. "There was a customer who we noticed a pattern that indicated some financial stress. The customer would have his car serviced on days that would allow him to use the service car for trips and weekends. He would even delay having the car serviced to insure he would have more time to use the service car."

As Sean noticed the pattern he thought, "His relationship wont last long." Speaking in regard to the customer's significant other who also became a customer. The woman had a great career and credit to match. Her boyfriend, the questionable customer, attempted to advise her on the best decisions to make. This would have been ideal if the gentleman was a "creditable" source. His credit score was substantially lower.

The couple eventually would separate over credit and finance, proving Sean correct. "We see it in this business all the time. He messed my credit up or she messed my credit up. Partners and spouses taking on cars that they can't afford or trying to get out of cars they shouldn't have had."

Our credit histories impact so many facets of our lives today. From credit cards and loans to employment and insurance. But why, why is it that the $53 cable bill that you could have paid 3 years ago, however, you were "making a point" is now causing you to have higher insurance, interest rates, and denials? Short answer, Risk.

So what does credit have to do with relationships? What can what you know about someone's credit history tell you about them? Short answer, risk. Short of obvious personal information, a lot. In fact, over the years as a credit underwriter, boyfriend, and as a consumer, I have learned and continue to learn the many correlations between credit histories and interpersonal relationships.

Let's start at the surface level, the actual score. In the last chapter, I mentioned that the Fair Isaac Company calculates a score for you, FICO score from credit data. Other companies such as Experian, Transunion, and Equifax also do the same. These companies are who we in the United States use for our credit reports and they have their own scoring systems also however, for the sake of this example we'll use the score that most lenders use, FICO. They have provided the breakdown which is also available on their website available at the end of the book in the "Resource" section. However, here is their calculation breakdown:

35% Payment History

30% Amounts Owed

15% Length of Credit History

10% New Credit

10% Credit Mix

This tells us how we pay based on history, late or on time. How much debt we currently carry. How long we've had credit or how much experience we have. What what type of credit we have, i.e. Mortgage, Credit cards, Student or Auto loans, etc.

From this are we balanced, experienced, or stressed? Do we honor our commitments? Again, as an underwriter in simplest terms, my job was to determine the relationship of the borrower and the bank. The score and report helped me to determine the likelihood of default.

From this information provided on the report let's say there was a pattern of late payments that started one month after the accounts opened. Those same accounts would then default after the 6th month. It is likely that borrower would continue this pattern with us upon approval. Especially if there are no other accounts that were satisfied. If we were to examine deeper we could possibly investigate this for fraud, however, we can save that for a different conversation. We will summarize this application decision as denial and agree does not honor commitments.

How would we relate this to dating? Aside from obvious of bad credit history, this person has a pattern of starting financial commitments with no intent of finishing. Some could argue what if something happened? True, they did make a payment or two. Yet, they opened other accounts and attempted to open others without satisfying defaulted accounts.

Now apply this scenario to a relationship, this is a habit that some couples learn in relationships at the wrong times, often when it is to late. For example, you meet this same borrower and are amazed by their charm, personality, and physically attracted to them. Months maybe even years go by and your relationship has reached a serious level. If you are not married, you both are either considering it or planning for it. One day they ask you to apply for this great offer for something they really want. You want love them so naturally, you want them to be happy. They've assured you they'll take care of the payment.

You've agreed, this is the first of several accounts that have been opened. Six months later, it is time to get a new home for any possible reason. That is when it happens, at the mortgage brokers office you receive the shock of your life. Your perfect credit history was just denied for your dream home. Your better half is not there with you, conveniently, they had an emergency at work.

I would love to say this was a figment of my imagination, however, I had a borrower that experienced this same ordeal. They didn't check their credit history often, only when they made large purchases because they paid everything on-time. They applied for the the card for their significant other and thought no more about it because it was for them and they were to pay for it, never to hear about it again until they met with the mortgage company. By then it was already in default and there were several accounts.

Conversely, with a conversation at the beginning of the relationship they could have learned about their payment habits and potential "risk" of the person that ruined their credit and dream of owning a home at the time.

This is simply one example and thing that credit can tell us about people and relationships. We can delve deeper and talk about the patterns as it relates to trust. Aside from things that may happen in life and I'm not immune to them, medical issues, natural disasters, layoffs, divorces, etc. Many things can affect a person's credit history. However, conversation should be the determining factor of the correlation between the person and their history.

When we talk about credit histories and its ability to show trust or lack thereof, it's those who intentionally don't pay or honor their commitments. Just like those who don't honor their relationship commitments intentionally, as in infidelity.

While this is not an exact science but it has been my experience that as creatures of habits if a person is not willing to honor their financial commitments, why would they commit to an interpersonal relationship? Again, not speaking of a person who has had challenges that caused credit issues. This person's other qualities typically will shine and you'll be able to determine in further conversation. This is valuable information that is worth the conversation to learn the potential mates spending and repayment habits. These things can offer insight into how they value and honor commitment.

My associate and I were talking in my office and we joked, "if they won't commit to keep their phone on, why would they commit to a relationship. People are building their lives with *pre-paid* people with *post-pay* expectations." That may be a little facetious, yet, the point is very real and clear. How can you expect someone who doesn't take something as serious as their finances or financial obligations to take your relationship serious?

Another item I looked at in correlation of credit history and interpersonal relationships was debt. Now I will admit I'm going out there with this one but bare with me it'll make sense. I mentioned the "Debt-to-Credit" percentage or "Utilization" previously. The formula is simply, total balance divided by total credit available (i.e. Credit available $10,000, balances $2,500, 2500/10000=.25 or 25% utilization). This says the borrower has good moderation of their credit spending of what's available to them. Key words in the last statement, MODERATION, AVAILABLE TO THEM.

Applying this to the dating world and reversing the ratio to say 75% utilization would say there may be an issue of moderation. Not to objectify anyone but let us equate credit card accounts to relationships for a moment for the sake of example. Total balance of the accounts is still $10,000 but it's broken up in 10 accounts or 10 relationships or 10 people you are seeing. You are 75% utilized, which means that your total balance in all accounts or relationships is $7,500.

Remember in my explanation of "Debt to Credit" in the previous chapter that as an underwriter, I viewed this as potential stress. Let's take away the financial aspect of the 10 accounts and equate the utilization to normal relationship or dating requirement, i.e. time, phone calls, walks, dates, gifts, etc. This means that you are 25% away from being completely maxed out of your ability "dating", in this example. If you are dating 10 people at one time "God bless you", I'm sure you can attest that this is taxing on you mentally, emotionally, and financially. Back to the financial example with 75% utilization you would only be $2,500 away from being maxed out of all of your credit lines. This is entirely to much potential stress which makes for potential risk, which without discussion and sufficient explanation leads to denial.

I stated, I was going out there but the point is one of the things that credit can tell us is moderation levels. In other words, how well the person moderates and how much will power they may have, if we want to get deeper. However, let us just look at moderation. Merriam - Webster defines moderation as *"An avoidance of extremes in one's actions, beliefs, or habits."* Lack of moderation is what seems to get people in trouble. Having a drink in moderation is not what causes problems. Maxing out your credit cards for special occasions, holidays, vacations, etc. with a plan to pay the balances off does not mean you have spending or credit problems. Living on credit cards, buying things well above your means, and maxing out credit cards with no record of why does however indicate a problem.

The key is moderation and I'm no different, I had to learn about moderation as it relates to several things in life. I believe there is a saying "Things are best served in moderation". It holds true because there are no after affects to whatever you receive or do. Be it food, alcohol, or spending, you don't face horrible sometime life altering repercussions when things are in moderation.

Dating is no different, how can you truly have the chance to know if the person you are dating is the one for you if you are spread out over 10? How can you pay down 10 cards from 75% if you are payments are spread out over 10? Of course there is a way but it will be taxing and stressful.

In the simplest form, it comes down to trust and finance. The word finance is not by any means to be mistaken for money, however, the ability to manage money or said finance. Merriam-Webster defines finance as "money or other liquid resources of a government, business, group, or individual." While defining credit as "a record of how well you have paid your bills in the past." Credit as it relates to relationships can tell us about our potential mates and life partners.

Chapter Five

"Seriously Relationships, Relationships, Seriously?"

It feels like, long gone are the days or so it seems when relationships were long lasting, built on trust, and security. The foundations of our households were built on the sanctity and union of the serious relationships that started them. For example, I can remember my grandparents. It seemed to be a pretty simple formula, he'd work she'd make the home and manage the finances.

Though at the time I didn't think to much of it, there was a lot of trust in what seemed so simple and everyday. What I mean is, she trusted him to leave home, work, and return with income. Enough to provide and sustain their lifestyle. He trusted her to care for the family, make the home, and manage his hard earned income without question. My grandmother worked early on in their relationship and collectively they made the decision for her to be a full-time homemaker.

There must've been something to their system, their union lasted 55 years, bore 4 beautiful children, 6 grandchildren, with all of their children going to college.

As I got older and began to experience life for myself, I began to experience some of the differences and similarities in their relationships and others, especially working in the banks. I learned how financially savvy my grandmother actually was and why she handled the finances.

Now to this day, no one will confirm or deny, but I'm pretty sure my grandmother was a day trader. I'm talking about before the "ETrades, Scottrades" and other online brokerages. She taught me about investing and the stock market.

This was my first indication that maybe I had some of these perceptions wrong about money, who made it, how it was made, and finally the term "homemaker".

Aside from from the finance component of their relationship, although it's a huge component in every relationship, every other component flowed smoothly that I can remember. Granted, I was young, but I'm pretty sure I would remember if not scarred if there were memories of my grandparents fighting or yelling. Fortunately, that was never the case.

I equate this to the huge component of finance being handled and addressed well before I was twinkle in my mother's eye. Assuming finance makes up 75% of relationships, 25% the rest, whatever that may be. If you address the 75% of what could go wrong in your relationship, look at all the time and energy you have to focus on the "whatever." Yes, let you minds and imaginations wonder. Letting your minds and imaginations wonder in a relationship strengthens it.

How great would it be to explore and learn new things with your partner and best friend? For instance, traveling exploring new places because, "hey," the budget allows it and it's what you both love to do and what you have in common. How about instead of fighting over bills or spending ours not talking and finding ways not to be in the same room or house, you spend hours making love with your significant other because they are the most beautiful person in the world to you. You're not stressed because your bills are under control because you both worked out a plan and system. You never noticed how beautiful he or she looks in this shade of "stress-free."

These are just some examples, but it's completely up to you, the point is, your relationship is amazing with the burden of stress lifted off of the both of you, and that is why relationships are long lasting.

"We have to dispute those beliefs of what we think finance in regard to marriage is and what it isn't. We have to have assigned roles, sometimes it's the man that's the financial planner and the woman is the provider, but this is 2016 and everybody has to work. However, the point is to be humble and share your weakness and say maybe I'm not good at math. An example of my wife and I, my wife is a control freak, she controls the finances. I get no shut off notices, always food in the fridge, if I want a toy, I tell her, she tells me when. So she's that person, me I provide I have the business, multiple streams of income I tell her, Girl just take this check" - Kier

Chapter Six

Three C's of ~~Credit~~ Love

So you're there, the point where you met that person who may be worth your time, love, affection, admiration, etc. What do you look for? Granted, I know we all may have our own specific tastes, likes, dislikes, etc. Let's examine deeper, let's talk about the foundation. Consider this, if they weren't attractive or they couldn't dress, they wouldn't have received your attention, right? If they didn't have a personality that kept your attention or stimulated your mind, they wouldn't even be in the running to be your man or woman, correct? So we don't need to discuss that.

What we do need to discuss however, is the proper tools and l things to look for to make the "approval", if you will. If you remember from earlier in the book, I stated I would teach you to be "Love Underwriters". I also mentioned that the best tool is communication.

The thing about communication is that you need to know 2 basic things, what message do you hope to receive or identify, and what message do you use to receive that message honestly and accurately. Meaning, how do I get them to tell me what it is I need to know without directly asking them in some cases. This can prevent setting them up to deceive you even it wasn't intentional. It also stops them from feeling uncomfortable and you as well. For instance, you wouldn't just come right out and ask, "How many people have you slept with?" while comparing your favorite wines. I mean I know people who have and do, maybe it works for them but for most people it doesn't.

So let's start with what information we hope to obtain in this line of communication. Going back to the world of credit underwriting, remember earlier in the book I mentioned credit underwriting or analysis is the first step of collections?

With that principle we approach the application knowing what we don't want. We don't want borrowers who don't honor their commitments. We don't want borrowers who don't have the ability to repay their loans or financial commitments to us. We are cautious with borrowers who are not stable.

This is from a lending standpoint, however,

look at its application to relationship environment. Would you want a mate that doesn't have a history of honoring their commitments? Would you want a mate that doesn't have the ability (maturity, mentality, health, etc.) to honor their commitment to you? Finally, would you want a mate that is not stable, without acceptable reason? Generally, the answer would be no. Remember again, without judgment, there may be a reason for certain answers. This is why communication is important, to fully understand what the answers are and why they may be.

We simplify this line of questioning with the acronym S.A.W.:

☐ **Stability** – Are they stable; do they know what they want out of life, are they working? What is their living situation? Do they have their own home or residence?

☐ **Ability** – Do they have the ability to commit or be in a relationship with you? Are they mature enough to be in the type of relationship you want? Do they have the mentality that is on your level? Do they think like you or how you feel you mate should think? Are they financial compatible with you? Not necessarily if they have a similar income as yours or not, but does their financial goals and management match yours? Are they mentally or emotionally attached to someone else or a past relationship? Are they still in a relationship?

☐ **Willingness** – Are they willing to commit or be in the same type of relationship you are looking for? What are their intentions with you? What are they looking for? Why aren't they in a relationship? Have they been in a relationship before? What happened in the previous relationship?

These questions are adaptive to your relationship goals and ideals in a partner. As long as they allow you to properly assess the foundation or the S.A.W. of your potential mate. I wish I could tell you what answers are acceptable but just as in lending from product to product and bank to bank, the criteria for approval is different. It comes down to what works for you and what you are willing to accept.

A few things I want to remind you is to, Communicate, have conversations. Believe it or not banks are not in business to deny applicants, although if you're on the receiving end of a denial, it can certainly feel that way. In that same manner you shouldn't set in your mind to find reason not to date or go to another level with this particular person. This is just a guide to cautiously move forward, to clearly know what it is you are getting involved with and manage your relationship accordingly.

Conversely, don't go into the situation to optimistic, ignoring red flags. The saying is "What happens in the wash eventually comes out in the rinse." This is no different, you can ignore flags such as; no consistent job history or never been in a relationship longer than 1 month. However, once you find out the reason for those things it will most certainly affect your relationship. Even in more relative circumstances, credit, you don't want to be in the situation like the mortgage borrower. Imagine yourself learning about the the red flag that you ignored at the worst possible time.

Remember from our discussion about stress and "fight or flight", the importance of knowing or at least, having an idea of how our future responds to stress? It also important to be honest with yourself how you respond to stress. If not, one of these situations could lead to a very stressful situation. These ultimately cause, in most cases relationship ending, situations.

We can see how situations like that can cause a major strain on relationships. Furthermore, why finance is the number one cause of divorce. Alternatively, we see how having conversations, understanding, and truly knowing your mate can help alleviate stress in relationships.

Industry-wide in lending, underwriters look at something called the "Three C's of Credit" to assess applicants. The Three C's", similar to "S.A.W." tells us foundational things about our applicants. In the case of this book, it tells us the foundational things about our potential mates.

The "Three C's" are:

> ☐ **Character or Credit History** – Tells us how a borrower managed their credit in the past and present to give us an idea of what they will do in the future. What kind of accounts do they

have currently or have they had? What is their payment history currently and previously? How often are they requesting new credit? Do they have a lot of inquiries? What type of inquiries do they have? Are they employed? If so, how long? If not, why not? What is their residence scenario? Do they rent, own, or live with relatives? How long have they lived there?

☐ **Capacity** – What is their income? What is their debt to income ratio? Do they have disposable income? Are they self employed or employed (this tells the frequency of income, self employed may not receive income depending on what happens with business while employed may be more dependable) What is their monthly expenses that may not be reported on the credit report? What are the terms and amount of what they are applying for? (For example, if it's a mortgage, how long is the term, 15,30, etc.? How much is the payment? If credit card, what is the max line?) How does the products applied for effect the applicants financial picture (Will the mortgage payment increase the debt to income ratio above 40%?)

☐ **Collateral or Capital** – How much does the applicant have in savings, retirement, investments, etc.? It applying for secured loan or product, how much is applicant using as a down payment? (I.e. Applicant is making a $5,000 down payment on new car.) If application is for a mortgage product, what is the property used for (i.e. Primary home, second, investment, etc.) How much equity is in the property? What is the Loan to Value? (How much is owed or will be owed vs. how much the home or property is worth?) What is the purpose of the product or loan? (Is it a cash-out refinance or a rate and term refinance? In other words, is the applicant looking to use equity in the home or simply lower the rate, payment, or change the term of the loan?)

You can see, it is more detailed with most of the answers coming form the application and credit report, yet, this still has the same purpose as S.A.W. Are they stable, are they able, and do they have willingness to pay or repay? Applying "The Three C's" to love, we would look in conversation to understand the character of the person we're considering to be our mate. We would also look at their capacity, are they able to fit us in their lives and share our goals? What is their collateral? Finally, do they have to support what they are saying?

For instance, you meet someone who says they want to be a doctor or lawyer, what are they doing to show that is true or they're serious? Are they in school? Are they complaining about student loans? Have they taken any number of exams or in any intern or residency programs?

How about they love your business acumen, and they blurt out, "Well I have my own business?" What do they have to show that is true besides a same day printed business card that "accidently" fell out of their pocket?

Asking them about said aspiration or goals, someone with an aspiration or goal that consumes that much of their life normally will talk in great detail about it to just about anyone who will listen. This is especially true for someone they are trying to impress.

I know starting any one of my businesses, I waited for the moment that someone would give me any indicator to talk about business. This isn't vanity in most cases or bragging. We are proud and passionate of what we are doing. With that being said, people who are that involved with an aspiration or goal should be experts or so it would sound to us unless, of course, we also are in the same industry or line of work. In either case, listen for inconsistencies in their explanation and stories.

When in doubt ask for proof. As an underwriter, especially with credit cards, we would often have people whose credit report did not match what they were saying or their application. We would at that point request proof of any thing from income to assets. "Ok Mr. John Doe, you make $2,000, 000 per year with $10,000,000 in the bank?" Meanwhile, Mr. Doe's credit report shows maxed out $500 credit cards with scattered late payments on a mortgage for $600 per month. While his application shows he owns his home outright with no payment.

While this is an extreme example, you can see why we would want to verify his income. I had a similar situation when an applicant had low credit lines and mortgage payments that didn't match what he was saying or his application. I requested proof, which was true and valid. It turned out, the gentleman never used credit. The credit on his file was all for his son. He placed everything in his name for his son and his son just couldn't handle the responsibility. Which is more than likely why the man had everything in his name for his son, because his son's credit was ruined.

The point, I would have never known if A. I didn't ask about it, B. I didn't request proof, and C. Most importantly, I didn't know the flags to look for that indicated something was wrong.

Chapter Seven

Dating in a Risky World

In a New York Time article that we were mentioned in on Christmas 2012, there was a line that read "Credit Scores are like the dating equivalent of a sexually transmitted disease test." That's sound a little extreme, however, when you think of what we go through in this world on a day to day basis, even as individuals, we would like to A. be protected and B. know who we are trusting with our lives and finances.

In relationships, we face a lot of challenges external and internally. In most cases the internal challenges are caused by the external and the past. What is the biggest culprit of these challenges? You guessed it, finances. It could be finance challenges of the past it could be something that's completely out of either one of your control but affects you both financially, but it causes strain on the relationship. A lot of times these relationships don't recover.

Think of a breakup, it could be one from your

past or someone's that you know. Now I pose these two questions, 1. Was the breakup over finances? Even if he or she cheated, think about the first argument or when you or the person this applies to first started to notice or feel discontentment in the relationship. Did something financial happen or change? Loss of job, unexpected bill, tragedy, large purchase, natural disaster, etc. Now that this is established, 2. Did you or the person this applies to say, "Man, they really changed, I've never seen he or she like this before. They're like a completely different person. etc." Remember, "fight or flight," or "acute stress response".

Let me say first, I'm sorry if I brought up painful memories. I promise, this was not my intention. I wanted you see how finances can affect relationships. Wait, it is not just finances, on to the second question. It's not that the person has changed, that person was there. You never saw how that person responded under that type of pressure or "stressor".

This is the same whether you were the cause of the financial issue or not. Think about the last chapter where we assessed the person's "Three C's" or "S.A.W." Within the either "Character" or even the "Ability" assessment, you could determine what type of person he or she really is if thing were to get bad. It all goes back to what happened with past relationships and are they mature and can their mentality handle a "serious relationship".

Those are surface level questions and evaluations, deeper would pertain to finances. Were you and this person financially compatible? Did you share the same financial goals? Did you determine who was stronger financially? By this I don't mean who made the most money, but who handle finances the best? By determining these things early on, you would be able to see how this person is under financially stressful conditions or if they would put you in a financially stressful situation.

Remember in the last chapter, I talked about "Collateral" in relationships? When in doubt, ask for proof. Now I don't mean ask them for their proof of income or assets, but at the point that you and this person are dating seriously or considering it, have "what if" conversations and simulations. This is where you can apply your self evaluation to theirs and see how they really respond to you. If you are truly a good fit. Call it "financial real world role-playing" and add some excitement in your relationship. Yes, I am being a little lighthearted, but in all seriousness have conversations about these matters and discuss what roles and actions you would take in such events. As my aunt would say, "see if it's really the deal for you."

For instance, use past situations if you've experienced them or if you haven't, use something from history. These could be anything from a job loss or loss of hours to natural disaster. This is also good for planning good things also not just negative scenarios.

Say for example you meet someone and you both determine that you want to have the Tudor style home with the white picket fence, matching Volvos, and 2.3 kids. I know it's not possible to have a third of a child, but I'm always reminded of those studies where they said "The average American household has 2.3 kids." Back to our example and your Tudor style home and perfect life. Because you have these things in common and you both get excited about it, why not plan it out.

Determine what it would take to reach that goal. Plan what roles each of you would take to reach it. Have fun with it, make a date night of it and create cute vision boards.

Doing this should help bring you two closer together and have your plan and dreams in-sync. This is part of "acting you dreams out with open eyes" ™ together. Even in the conversations and simulations with negative scenarios, you two should be brought closer together and you will prepare each other for such events, should they arise.

These exercises have no right or wrong answers or solutions. They are simply exercises to determine opportunities to improve upon, as well as assess who's more equipped to handle what.

For example, you may be the one who is better with money management. You may have already knew this but now your partner sees this in a real world setting and why it's important. Your partner may be more inspirational or motivational. They may be the voice you need in a situation to keep you calm and focused on the goal or surviving what ever negative situation may have arisen. Either way, by these strengths and weakness being exposed proactively. This is much better than learning about this in the middle of a crisis or after you both impulsively decide to buy the Tudor style home or the 2 Volvos while living in their parent's basement.

This is a great time to talk about something I'm asked about in different countries, languages, settings, media formats, etc. by friends, family, journalists, and even celebrities. Credit scores, when to talk about them. There is really no definitive answer to this question. It truly depends on you, your relationship goals, and the person you're dating or considering dating.

For the record, I wouldn't say ask someone their credit score randomly in the middle of the nightclub after 3 drinks and dancing to Drake's "Hotline Bling".

Why, simply because it's not a good setting for a serious conversation. Not that "Hotline Bling" is not a great song to get telephone numbers to. People may say but your dating site matches people based on that and they're essentially exchanging their credit scores before knowing each other. Well, not quite, the difference is my members come to my site looking for serious relationships and they want to match with singles who have same financial mindset as theirs.

So when is a good time to discuss it? I would say when you feel comfortable that this is someone you feel you'd consider having a serious relationship with. It could be "love at first site" it could be 10 dates in. It truly depends on you and your chemistry with that person and how they align with your relationship and life goals. Nonetheless, this discussion is important in determining not only is this person financially compatible with you but are they compatible with you overall.

This person may make a million dollars per year but have horrible credit. It's up to you to determine why that is the case. Maybe they are too busy to pay their bills on time. Maybe they just have all around horrible money management skills. Maybe their credit suffered a major hit from a divorce, business loss, catastrophe. Most importantly, if this person is worth it, maybe you can help with your superior money management skills.

Thing of the yin yang sign and the saying "opposites attract", you may not make as much as this person, but you have perfect credit. Think of what kind of power couple you could be, filling each others voids. Listen to me, I just played matchmaker with you and an imaginary person, damn, I'm good.

Pardon me for my moment of vanity, just wanted to make sure you are still with me. Even if a person doesn't have the best credit in the world per se. It can tell you a lot. Not just negative things, what if it told you positive things? What if someone with a marginal, average, or below average score told you things that possibly makes the deal? No, I'm not crazy and this is not one of my sarcastic joking moments. First, it would depend on you, what you are looking for, and your relationship goals. Second, you would have to converse and really delve into why the person's score is in this range.

My older cousin used to say to me, "I'd go to war with a soldier in a tattered uniform before a soldier in a new uniform any day." He told me this years ago, as I prepared to write this book, I thought about it. That saying means that the soldier in the tattered uniform has gone to war and returned. The soldier is war tested, has been to battle and returned to tell about it, knowing what to expect and most importantly how to survive.

Let's apply this to dating, sure a person with perfect credit may look amazing, but it also may say that they may not have experienced some of the hardships that may come. Now, I'm not saying that anyone with perfect credit has never had any thing bad happen to them, furthermore, I'm not wishing anything bad happen to anyone. If I had it my way, this would be a perfect world where we never experienced any hardships. Unfortunately, that's not the world we live in. There are some people with great credit or perfect credit that have experienced worse things than we could imagine but they recovered and they remained consistent since that recovery. Remember, most things can legally stay on your credit file for 7 years, some 10 depending what it is, what it's current status is or was, and how often that information is being updated.

People ask me about credit all of the time and another misconception is about the length items stay on the credit report. Someone will say to me, "Niem, I've had this account on my credit report that's hurting my credit." I'll naturally ask about the item. The common response is similar to this, "Well, it's an account I haven't had in years, at least 7." To which I'd simply inquire was it paid off and when? This is where the misconception comes in, "Well no but it's 7 years old, so it should come off right?" Unfortunately, that's not correct, it 7 years from the last date the company reported, at which point the credit reporting agency should remove it. If the bill was never paid and the creditor reports every month for 7 years it was not paid, it will continue to report until 7 or 10 years from when they last reported. This is the same if they sold it to a collection agency. The item will stay on your file for 7 years from the last date reported.

Now if there is a true inaccuracy, you should take the steps to dispute the inaccuracy. We will cover this a little later and I will include resources at the end of the book.

Getting back to the point, take a moment and think about in your lifetime what disasters you may have experienced or could have experienced. Once again I'm not trying to dredge up painful memories, simply making a point. If you weren't of age to be affected financially or in a region that would have affected you, imagine for a moment if you were. How many times would that have been in your lifetime? Exclude health issues, just think of natural disasters, terrorist attacks, recession, etc. In my lifetime there has been 9/11 and the economic meltdown of 2008. 9/11 affected my first job. Those are just two that I'll disclose for the benefit of this example. Those two were huge, they affected economies all over the world. If I were to name all the things that went or can go wrong, this would be the guide of disasters. I'm sure we can agree that unfortunately, we live in a world where things go wrong that affect us all.

When someone has a score that is marginal or average they have been through something. It reflects that they may have experienced financial stress caused by personal issue, i.e. job loss, health, etc. or external issues natural disasters, economic disasters, acts of terror, etc. How can this be a dealmaker? Well, it would depend on the conversation. First question, why is the score so low? What are your plans to correct it? Depending on the answer to these questions and the other factors that you are considering about this person, this should be a dealmaker or breaker.

Remember in my example a little while back about the application not coinciding with the credit report? This is similar, does this person show signs of recovery? Did they tell you they have a 500 credit score but they seem to to make decision that reflect poor money management? For instance, they live with their parents to recover from whatever financial catastrophe, i.e. divorce, job loss, etc. Yet you notice they're either at the club every weekend spending money like they're a celebrity. Are they more focused on getting a new car than moving out of their parent's basement? Is he or she king or queen Midas payday weekend then the next week they're on a mysterious diet because they can't afford to eat? Chances are they haven't learned their lesson and they should be a relationship denial.

However, if they never go out and they are saving money every where they can, decided to build a business so they'll never be put in the situation of losing their job again and they monitor their credit score like people watch football scores, it is safe to say, they've learned their lesson.

You may say, "That's good, they've learned their lesson, but what does that mean for me?" Remember my cousin's saying, well, this soldier has returned from war with the credit report being their tattered uniform.

When things happen that we hope wont but prepare if they do, this person has been through it. They could be a resource of everything from the feelings of how to deal with changes that may occur to the steps of recovery. They are also conditioned on what to reinforce, this time with vengeance.

Think about fire, if you've never been burned by it, yet, you never dared touch it why? Because someone told you not to and the consequences of your actions. I can assure you the reason we know and we're told not to touch it is because someone somewhere played with it and got burned. They began to tell people or people who witnessed said, "Hey man, you might not want to touch that, Johnny did and it messed him up."

It is one thing to hear something is bad and can happen but it's completely different to actually hear it and have it reinforced by someone who has been through or witnessed it. Conversely, your good habits can rub off on them. You can possibly reinforce the benefits of having good credit and money management skills. They would see their personal goal in real time.

The goal is to be prepared for what may come at you, your mate, and your relationship in this risky world of unexpected circumstances. Our relationships should enhance us, make us stronger, smarter etc. This is why it is important that we are selective when it comes to choosing who we want to be with. This is because they are us and we are them. They may have to fight with you against odds, adversity, tragedy, and external forces that may come your way.

I've always been taught that your home is your safe zone. You fight all day to conquer goals, act out dreams, prove yourself in a world that seemingly may be against you. But home is where you rest and recover. How can you survive if you have to fight in the world and in your home? How can a relationship survive if someone is fighting or seemingly fighting against you? You can't, and this is a reason for relationship terminations.

People try to carry to much on their shoulders in a relationship. No matter the intention, whether it is pride or love, whether it's genuine or just to say they did it. Relationships are 50/50 not 60/40, 80/20, 90/10, or any thing less than even. Finances in a relationship are no different. I can't stress this enough, this is not about asset value or income but how it's handled. It doesn't matter how the $100,000 comes in the house, what makes the difference is how it goes out. The money management is what's important and what helps or hurts it, whether it's past, present, or future. The key is communication about the past, present, and future.

Chapter Eight

Love, Life, and Finance: It's all a rollercoaster ride, Buckle up!

People close to me would tell you that I never have a day that is all bad or all good. My days much like life, love, and finances are a rollercoaster. Ups and downs, twists and turns dips and dives. This doesn't bother me, I'm used to it, more importantly, I'm prepared.

But how do you prepare for a day that can be one extreme to the next? Well to answer this question, I resort back to the wisdom of my cousin. He said, "Nye, you have to be even keel." He said to keep a calm disposition with everything no matter how good or bad. There are days when I would receive multimillion dollar offers and days when I would lose tons of money. There are days when I'm doing press around the world and then there are days when meetings, speaking engagements, and other important events get canceled last minute. I used to be a live wire and if you were around me you would hear it. This was no way to live or have others living around me.

This personal example is that is to display that

sometimes the best preparation is to adjust our expectations. However, to adjust your expectations, you have to first know what you expect. Furthermore, if these expectations involve another person they must know what you expect of them and vise – versa.

I hear things all the time from random people about how "so and so" let them down. Yet, "so and so" didn't know what was expected of them. How could they possibly know prevent from disappointment if they didn't know what was expected?

Would you date someone knowingly who would openly break an expectation or disappoint you? No, of course not. Going back to the credit report and what it tells us, remember it tells us how a person honors commitments. The banks and institutions, however, have to let the borrower know what the commitments and expectations they have of you honoring those commitments, correct? They do every chance they get from the application, to the statement, to the collection call should it get to that point. Nonetheless, they let you know, or else they wouldn't be able to collect on the agreement, in fact, there would not be any. There would simply be a bank giving you money.

My lawyer explained to me an agreement or contract as a record of expectations. He said this is true no matter if it's the operating agreement for a corporation or an agreement between parties doing business together. This way the parties involved always know what's expected of them. The same is true with your card member agreement with your credit card provider. In fact, you reinforce that agreement every time you sign the merchant copy of the receipt. The next time you make a purchase look at the little sentence normally below the signature line. It read something similar to this:

I agree to pay above total pursuant to the card issuer
agreement

So what does this have to do with relationships, dating, and love? Did I lose you yet? I hope not, if so don't worry, I'm bringing it back around right now. With all the ups and down in love, life, and finances, shouldn't you know what to expect from your mate? Shouldn't they know what to expect from you? No, I'm not going to say have them sign a contract. Although, it's not to bad of an idea. It can be fun, a love contract, outlining the expectations of your relationship. Either way, the expectation should be clearly discussed and outlined. However, be realistic and fair remember, "even keel". Remember relationships should be 50/50, don't place an expectation on someone that you couldn't live up to yourself.

Once your expectation has been set in place and outlined, communicate them to each other, remind each other. I'm not saying become like the bank leaving little notes around the house or making them sign for every act or gift of love and kindness with a line below that says:

I agree to fulfill my expectation pursuant to the relationship agreement.

Don't send statement and make collection calls either. Just make simple reminders, that is if they're needed. This protects the relationship from internal forces and challenges. When the core is solid and unified external forces are less powerful against the relationship.

I sensed that you felt an example coming. Here it is, let's assume you have an expectation that your significant other tells you when they are approached by another person looking to date them. They do and you know everything, in fact you two have such great communication, that you joke about it. You then receive information about this person that approached your significant other. You are not shocked, in fact you expected it because you and your mate already discussed it.

Conversely, let us say he or she never told you and you receive this same info. You now begin to wonder why did your mate not tell you about this? Because the expectation wasn't fulfilled, there's room for external forces to bring problems and break down the relationship.

I took a different approach, nonetheless, you can see the importance of communication and expectations. When setting expectations again be mindful of for whom you're setting expectations. For instance, if you know your mate is not good with money, don't set an expectation that has a reliance on money management. If you do, you are getting in the rollercoaster of love with no seatbelt. It's almost as if you're asking that person to disappoint you. Help your mate and guide them to understand as they grow your expectation of them should grow also.

Remember the role playing exercises we talked about previously? Setting expectations and creating the love contract can be a role play exercise. The goal is to make you both stronger individually and as a couple while preparing your relationship for the ups and downs of life and love. This also allows you to really get to know each other, the things that make you happy and conversely your dislikes.

You both knew what it took to get together and start the relationship. You got passed the stage of favorite colors, wines, foods, etc. What about pet peeves, annoyances, stressors? Why find out at the point when they're annoying you or you're annoying them? Why not find out proactively and learn to avoid it?

When you open a credit card, in your card member agreement, you learn that if you don't make your payment by your due date there is a late fee. You know that if you send in a check that is not honored and returned, there is a returned check fee. You know that once your payment is thirty days past due it is reported to the credit bureau and it affects your credit score. Why do you know this? Because these things are outlined in the expectations set in the card member agreement.

Some of us are more familiar with what banks and companies expect from us than our mates and life partners. Does that seem right? Some of us apply the same principles of honoring commitments and expectations to all relationships and get along just fine. Some of us don't honor any commitments at all and wonder why we suffer in life and feel the entire world is against us.

In my first book, "Daydreaming Mogul's Guide Vol. 1: Daydreams and Success" I discussed "Luck". Not the mythical luck, such as charms and rabbits' feet. I explained that luck is when preparation meets opportunity. If you are prepared for opportunities to arise, you more than likely will have a positive out-come. With that being said, relationships take luck. Relationship need preparation for not just the downs in love, life, and finance, but the ups as well.

Why should you be prepared for the "ups"? Well up signifies as change in direction. The key word is change, whether it is moving in together, marriage, addition to the family, additional income, lottery winnings, retirement, etc. Whatever it is or can be positive, it is change from the normal life you may have experienced. Lack of preparation can turn even the most positive situation into a negative situation.

Once again the easiest way to be prepared is to set reasonable "even keeled" expectations. Set these expectations of yourself as well as your mate. This way you will know "If this then that, if that then this." You and your mate will be lucky in love on the rollercoaster of love, life, and finance...

Chapter Nine

Good Credit is Sexy!

On a radio interview some time ago I had in Florida with David Holland. He asked me, "Is credit, good credit sexy?" Let's talk about this, finally we get to the main course of this book, the sexiness of credit. People often laugh and are puzzled when they hear my websites tagline "Where Good Credit is Sexy." This is because at first glance we don't look at credit as something sexy. We look at credit as something boring. Numbers, bills, responsibilities, credit scores and reports. What could possibly be sexy about that?

"You make good money and your credit is good. You are able get what you want when you want it. You're confident and it shows in your stride. The same works for relationships, if both of you have good credit that's a major worry that's alleviated. Leaving more time to focus on what's important, the relationship and each other." – Sean Johnson Porsche Delaware

And that's sexy, let's take away the scores and numbers and look at responsibilities. How do you look at a person who takes control of their responsibilities? A man or woman who confidently moves through life taking care of their business without worry because they honor every commitment. In fact, they have the maturity not to take on commitments that they don't have the capacity, capital, or character to honor. Their word is their bond, if they say it they mean it. If they can do something they say it and if they can't they honestly say that they can't.

There is no room or time for those type of games in their life because they are busy enjoying all that life has to offer without the stress of consequences from not honoring commitments. Is that not sexy? How sexy is it that you know that you can depend on that person if you ever need them? If you call them, you know without a doubt they will be there. If they can't you never doubt them because they never lied, that's not in their character. This is good credit and this is why good credit is sexy.

Is this not an attractive quality to have in a mate? Someone who is dependable, honest, and reliable. Someone who honors all of their commitments and will never take on more than they can handle.

Someone who is man or woman enough to say "No". Someone who understands and takes things in moderation.

This is attractive to banks and lenders also this is your applicant who receives the pre-approved credit card offers and loans as well as the non-solicited credit limit increases. The person who walks on the car lot and leaves with whatever they want with simply a signature.

This was an uncle of mine; he was so proud of that. I remember when I went to finance my first car. That bank wanted "blood" and my uncle thought it was so comical. He said "You'll get here one day." I didn't understand until I was older. I was risky, I never had any credit good or bad, so the bank had no idea who I was. Would I honor my commitment? Was I sexy or ugly, credit wise? So they need proof of everything and a co-signer. My uncle told me about how the dealer would call him every 2 years or so and send him cars and just have him come in to sign for them. This was because he was "sexy" to the banks. He had developed and proved his file over the years. He had every type of trade, mortgages, credit cards, car loans. He paid everything on time and never applied for anything he didn't feel the need. He lived in moderation at his means. He wouldn't co-sign for me, so I guess he didn't think I was "sexy" either.

Think as if it were a blind date, you have no idea who this person is that you are about to meet. You haven't seen them nor do you have any mutual friends. They tell you they are the perfect man or woman and they want to be with you. How can you believe that? What do you use to validate this is true or false?

Hopefully by now you can see where I'm going with this and why I've developed "Credit Score Dating". The principles that we've discussed up to this point are tools that you can use to help you in such a situation. Of course, that and meeting someone on creditscoredating.com. Yes, I had to plug my site, I think I did good this entire time. In any case, being serious again, understanding the correlation between credit, love, and interpersonal relationships can help to protect your heart.

What other ways are good credit sexy? What

about my cousin's saying we talked about a little while back, the soldier in a tattered uniform? While granted, you may find soldiers sexy or people in uniform for that matter. How about the qualities of someone who have experienced things and recovered? Someone who may have experienced financial hardships or stress and made a recovery, which is now reflected positively in their credit score and report. Is this sexy, resilience?

Personally, I love to see a woman who doesn't let life or situations beat her down. Even when things get tough she bounces back and comes back stronger. This is especially true when considering a life partner.

We mentioned in the previous chapter that life, love, and finances, are a rollercoaster ride. With all the ups and downs, it would be beneficial to have a partner who would be tested in these situations and can handle them. While writing this, a song comes to mind my mother used to sing to me, "When the Going Gets Tough, the Tough Gets Going", by Billy Ocean. The song appeared in the Michael Douglas movie, "The Jewel of the Nile". The movie was an action and adventure movie that remains one of my favorites to this day. It features Kathleen Turner as the damsel in distress, if you will.

I mention this movie and song for a reason. If you think about serious relationships, they are like movies. Just as in movies there are always climaxes, which makes the movie interesting. There are good guys and bad guys, heroes and heroines. Has there ever been a movie where the hero has come away unscathed? Has there ever been a movie where the hero has never seen any action? No, Of course not, that makes the film more realistic and believable. Also, there is a attractive quality in a hero or heroine that is experienced. How sexy is a person who can take the lead and does it well? I don't think it's attractive for someone not knowing and trying to lead. It's also sexy for someone not to fold under pressure but stand up and rise to the occasion. People are only able to do this with experience.

Chapter Ten

"Bringing the Sexy Back"

We talked about the "sexiness of credit" as well as some of the challenges of credit or credit that's not "sexy". Let me further iterate that a having bad credit shouldn't stop you from dating. Whether, you have bad credit or the person you're dating, this does not have to be a deal breaker. The point that you should have noticed throughout the book, or the as DJ Khaled would say, "Major key" is communication.

Let's talk about if you or your mate has bad credit from any various reason. As I'm often asked, "How do I bring my credit's sexy back? It all begins at the core, that is knowing where you or they stand and why. Once you make that determination, you are able to start addressing the issues. Much like my response to that question, I pose the question, "How can I fix a house if I don't know what's wrong with it or how it became damaged?"

Even if the credit was damaged from lack of caring, the fact that you or they want to correct the credit is a great sign. This shows acceptance, account-ability, and responsibility. These are mature qualities personally as well as in a relationship.

Take the time to revisit the problems that may have occurred that led to the credit file. Credit as we discussed earlier, as it relates to the score is mea-sured by several factors. Take a look at your file and see which factor is causing the most trouble to your score.

With the advancement of technology, a person can get their score and the factors that effect them on their phones. There are many sources to get this, from the credit reporting agencies to your bank like Capital One and their CreditWise product.

Just as in repairing your credit, similarly you can turn that relationship denial to an approval. Even if a person is ready to be denied for things unrelated to credit. If you find they have something that both-ers you about them or vise-versa, discuss what it is or how it originated. Is this something that can be repaired? This could be anything from little quirks that you don't like to major things such as commitment issues.

If you or they have money management issues that have led to bad credit. Talk about that issue, why does it exist? Is there anything that can be changed? Living above means, not saving, etc. How willing are you or they willing to work to correct the issue?

If the credit issue is because of debt, why? Is there a way to plan to eliminate the debt more aggressively? Is more debt being accrued at the same time? If the credit issue is payment related, why are payment not being made on time? Why weren't they paid on time in the past? Is there or was there a shortage of income issue? Can a stricter budget be put in place? Is there a budget established at all?

These are examples of places to begin in getting credit "sexy" again. Focus on the behavioral things and controls that may cause credit issues. We all know the definition of insanity, so it seems because most of us do insane things by definition. That is, doing the same thing repeatedly expecting different results. Much like other problems that we may face, the solution lies in us most cases.

I mentioned before that there are cases where there are inaccuracies on the credit report that may have an affect on your score. Like the other issues, you wont know unless you review your file periodically. If there is an inaccuracy, the reporting bureau has processes established for you to dispute them. There are also agencies such as Lexington Law or Creditrepair.com that can assist in this. These companies will also be available in the resource section of this book.

.

Chapter Eleven

Finally, For Love or Credit?

So we've made to the end, hopefully you've made to the relationship that you deserve. If your credit wasn't sexy, hopefully, it is now. So now what? I've been asked, "are they with me for love or credit?" In fact, some people ask if the site attracts people to other singles for solely the purpose of credit. I would love to say there aren't people who are looking simply for that.

Unfortunately, this is not a perfect world and there are dishonest people. There are people who use people for everything from sex, money, and in this case, credit. This is for you to determine and protect your heart, credit, etc.

Your heart and your credit are very valuable, so you should always treat the two as such. Banks and lending institutions rely on analysts, underwriters, credit bureaus, etc. to mitigate the risk of loss. You should do the same and this is why I've written this guide. I want to arm you with a resource and tools as a "Love Underwriter" to underwrite the potential candidates vying for you heart and love.

Hopefully not your credit or anything material and superficial. You are an amazing person and you have and if someone is chasing after your looks, money, or credit, they are missing out and that's on them. They are missing out. Your value lies in your what's beneath the surface.

A beautiful friend of mine said, "I'm working on me so I have more to bring to the table than just my looks. Looks fade and material things don't last forever. But the things that make me internally, like my love, my heart, and my mind last forever."

When you're confident in you and your capability to love because you love yourself, you have the ability to love on your terms confidently. Just as if you have good credit, you can pretty much buy whatever you want, when you want. You can freely make these purchases confidently without fear or denial or excessive verification.

Typically, people who have good credit are disciplined not to buy things and buy things without reason or cause. Similarly, people who love themselves don't settle or jump in and out of relationship just because. They know what they want out of relationships and wait to get it. This is because they know their value, they know what they "bring to the table."

This may be from trial and error, whether it was work on themselves that needed to be completed or adjusting their expectations of others. Once again, you can't appreciate the best if you never experienced the worst. This goes for you, relationships, other people, work, credit, finances, etc.

Let's talk about love, "Love looks not with the eyes, but with the mind. And therefore is winged Cupid painted blind." William Shakespeare stated in "A Midsummer Night's Dream." With that saying no matter how powerful and potent it may feel, true love is smart. "Love is that condition in which that happiness of another person is essential to your own." Robert A. Heinlein stated in "Stranger in a Strange Land."

From this I take that we need to be smart in love and prepare ourselves to make sure we are able to keep our significant other happy. Adding stress is not happiness. Fighting over finances and receiving denials for the things we want and need is not happiness.

This is the sexiness of credit, just as I explained to David Holland, "Security is sexy." Being secure that when problems arise even if we don't have the resources to solve, we have each other thinking on the same level. We are compatible in every capacity, including finance. We are secure and confident as a couple to make purchases, not just any purchase but the right purchases that wont affect us or our relationship. It's sexy to be with someone who love you enough to love smart and work for our happiness.

I'm a proponent of "Love". In reality, I'm what some would call a "hopeless romantic." I've learned however, just as Shakespeare stated, love is smart. I wanted to find a solution to the problem that plagues most relationships, finance.

Everyone needs true love; it feeds you more than any nourishment; you feel full in the presence of love. But there's a vast difference between love and true love. True love knows no depth. It's an endless tunnel that sweeps you up in the whirlwind and you're never quite free from it. It stays with you. And you hope this person will too. Falling in love is similar to falling in a big pool of warm chocolate. It's exciting, warm, and engulfing.

Falling in love is probably the best thing that can emotionally happen to a human being. It's a wonderful feeling. It's euphoric, the high that you never want to come down from. You're happy, at peace, and satisfied with your partner. No, that is an understatement, this is "the one". "The one" you've dreamed of, the one you dream with, the one you dream for and act those dreams and fantasies out with.

There really isn't anything better – emotionally – than falling in love. In fact, it affects us physically and mentally as well. The irony is that it sometimes causes us to make "goofy" mistakes. I like to call it the "Hitch effect". Yes, Hitch, like the movie starring Will Smith. If you've seen it, remember how he was perfect with his words, actions, and guidance, that is, until he fell in love himself. That's when he made his mistakes which was comical to watch. However, I find truth in it, we may be the best wordsmiths, planners, organizers, etc. So well put together, until we meet our match, our true love and "fall". We become tripped up, tongue-tied, and even down right "stupid". It's really intriguing the way the heart, body, and mind works. I like to think it's our way of showing "the one" our flaws so they know what and who they are receiving with no filter. So they can accept us for us, if they are our "True Love" they should reveal theirs as well and we find a certain peace within this bond of calamity.

It's really indescribable like the feeling of creating a child. You're passionate, caring, and more protective of your partner. You want them all to yourself. It feels like you could live with this feeling forever. You change and become a better person, for that person. In fact, you become a part of that person as they become a part of you. Aspiring to live as one, flaws and all happily ever after.

My daughter, Aunye, has developed the pattern of

doing all of her work, projects, etc. from hardest and most time consuming to the least. She also attacks the project that would be the most difficult immediately. For instance, if the assignment is due at the end of the month while being assigned in the beginning, she will work it to completion the day it's assigned. This allow her time to make little changes and perfect it with out haste. She's a bit of a perfectionist but she gets it honestly.

I looked at this and said this is smart, she said, "Daddy, it just makes sense, to make get the tough stuff done first so I'm not stuck or waiting until the last minute. I'm able to get all my work done correctly without rushing to have more time to do what I want to do." There something to this, not just because my daughter is an honor student consistently on the honor roll. Because if we apply her strategy to life and relationships, how much stress can we eliminate? How much time will we have to enjoy and learn ourselves and each other?

In a relationship the same is true, this is why I've spent years perfecting the algorithm to attack the biggest problem in relationships. This is why I have written this book. Let's address the issue or potential issue in the beginning so our relationships can grow.

Geraldo Rivera, stated in an interview that we did together,

"You're a young man or woman you want to get married, you meet someone you like. You begin to hook up and get serious and you find out that he or she has $75,000 in college loans outstanding. So your life is starting off in a handicap, not only are you taking on the person, you're also taking on a real financial burden."

In a news segment that we were on together, John Bussey of the Wall Street Journal, stated:

"That's what this is really about right? This is about kind of getting one more indicator of the other person's values. It's not just seeing if their solvent. It's a kind of generalized indicator of their values."

To answer the question titling the chapter, "Is it for love or credit?" The answer is both, use the credit as a tool to love smart and protect your partner and insure your happiness together. That is the sexiness of credit.

Resources

I've compiled some contacts to assist you in either keeping you credit sexy or making it sexy. Also, I've included some contacts of government agencies if you have trouble along the way. Credit Reporting Agencies:

Equifax Credit Information Services
Equifax Credit Information Services, Inc
P.O. Box 740241
Atlanta, GA 30374
www.equifax.com

Disputes:
Equifax Information Services, LLC.
P.O. Box 740256
Atlanta, GA 30348
Phone
866 349-5191

Experian PLC
P.O. Box 2002
Allen, TX 75013
www.experian.com
888 397-3742

Disputes:
P.O. Box 4500
Allen, TX 75013

Transunion

TransUnion LLC
2 Baldwin Place
P.O. Box 1000
Chester, PA 19016
www.transunion.com
800 888-4213

Disputes
Online:
https://dispute.transunion.com
Phone:
800-916-8800
Monday - Friday
Hours: 8 am – 11 pm EST
Closed on major U.S. holidays

Free Annual Credit Report:

Your rights to your free annual credit reports_Federal law requires each of the three nationwide consumer credit reporting companies - Equifax, Experian and TransUnion - to give you a free credit report every 12 months if you ask for it.

https://www.annualcreditreport.com

Credit and Financial Counselors

Financial Counseling Association of America (FCAA)
611 Pennsylvania Avenue, SE
#1600
Washington DC 20003-4303

www.fcaa.org
Phone: 866 694-7253
Credit Scores and Report Monitoring

Credit Karma
www.creditkarma.com

Credit Sesame
www.creditsesame.com

Quizzle
www.quizzle.com

Credit.com
www.credit.com

Fair Issac Corporation (Fico)
www.myfico.com

Capital One CreditWise
http://creditwise.capitalone.com

Discover Credit Scorecard
www.creditscorecard.com

Government Contacts

Federal Trade Commission

Federal Trade Commission

600 Pennsylvania Avenue, NW
Washington, DC 20580
Telephone: (202) 326-2222
www.ftc.gov

Consumer Financial Protection Bureau

Consumer Financial Protection Bureau
PO Box 4503
Iowa City, IA 52244
(855) 411-CFPB | (855) 411-2372
www.consumerfinance.gov

About The Author

Niem Green, also known as "The Daydreaming Mogul," is an entrepreneur, writer, motivational speaker, and consultant. Born in Philadelphia, PA, he spent 10 years in the financial sector specializing in lending, risk analysis, and project management. Green would later go on to make a name for himself in the field of dating and as a published author.

Niem, or "the Mogul," cites the ability to "act his dreams out with open eyes," as one of the primary factors to his success.

In 2009 he released "The Daydreaming Mogul's Guide Vol. 1 Daydreams and Success. The book explored his philosophy on how to achieve one's desires through the power of daydreaming. His books are available in over 100 countries through 50,000 retailers.

Green Walk Media is a multimedia subsidiary of Green Walk Industries that offers music, book, television, and film properties. Green Walk has established a recording studio in New Castle, DE to accommodate its music branch.

Niem owns the revolutionary and innovative site creditscoredating.com where users pursue romantic partners with an emphasis on desired credit score standards. Niem and his credit score dating site have been featured on NBC's "The Today Show," in addition to Fox, the New York Times, Reuters, ABC and many more major outlets globally.

A TV series called "Credit Score Dating" is being produced by Niem's Green Walk Media Group. The show will match couples based on credit scores and put them in real life scenarios to test the importance of financial responsibility in successful relationships.

Niem's passion for helping others and spreading his "open eyes" philosophy led to the creation of the "Young Daydreamers Foundation", which has recently partnered with The United Way. The current initiative of the foundation is the program Niem created, "I Have a Story to Tell." The aim of the program is to promote literacy by helping children in local schools and community centers create their own books. Besides improving their creative writing skills and reading comprehension, the program equips the kids with the necessary tools to achieve both short and long-term goals.

About Creditscoredating.com

What is Credit Score Dating?

Even Cupid wants to know your credit score, stated an article in NY Times. Credit scores are derived from a complex formula that weighs factors such as outstanding debt, payment history and new credit lines. The three-digit number is used to predict the likelihood of delinquency on obligations from credit card bills to a mortgage. Knowing your partner's credit situation helps members prepare for their futures with open eyes.

For many singles, bad credit can be a deal breaker when finding love. A recent study reveals that 20% of men and 30% of women between the ages 21- 34, say they won't marry someone with a poor credit score. Most respondents also say money management skills are just as important as looks when deciding whether someone is worth pursuing. While 57% of men say that credit scores play into their dating decisions, a staggering 75% of women said they consider the numerical rating. Within the last 6 years, dating based on financial stability and credit score ratings have become very popular in the American culture.

Who is CreditScoreDating.com?

CreditScoreDating.com allows members looking for serious dating to join for free and find compatible mates. Founder, Niem Green, saw a gap in the dating industry and the idea that credit scores are an indicator of how well someone handles commitment and honors agreements led to the creation of this online dating site.

When the site first launched in 2006, most of the members were in their 40s and, according to Green, often had relationships end because of financial issues. Following the financial crisis, the site experienced a surge in membership and a decline in the average age of members. Now CreditScoreDating.com has over 180,000 members using the online dating portal and a "significant percentage" are in their 20s and 30s.

Why CreditScoreDating.com?

Experts say smart singles are now seeking out websites that help match couples based on their credit scores. Knowing your mate's credit score and financial situation is very important before making life changing decisions. But no matter how important it may be, it can be an awkward topic to broach. CreditScoreDating.com allows you to choose your mate responsibly with out the hassles of wasted time on dates that lead no where.

9 780988 965904